THE CRUEL RADIANCE OF WHAT IS

THE CRUEL RADIANCE OF WHAT IS

SELECTED AND NEW POEMS
ANNETTE ALLEN

Negative Capability Press 2019
Mobile, Alabama

The Cruel Radiamce of What Is: Selected and New Poems
Copyright © Annette Allen, 2019

Cover painting by Melissa Day
Photography by Dean Lavenson
Author photo by Lisa Schonburg
Design by Jonathan Weinert

Library of Congress Control Number: 2018913980

ISBN: 978-0-9986777-9-8

Negative Capability Press
62 Ridgelawn Drive East
Mobile, Alabama 36608
(251) 591-2922

www.negativecapabilitypress.org

Contents

Foreword   ix

I: PLACE

Late   3
Beverly Drive   4
Between Piano and Door   6
Stillness   8
Portrait   10
Phone Call at the MacDowell Colony   11
Staying On   12
Severing Old Beliefs   13
The Dark Continent   15
Die Vermissten   17
German Cities   19
After The Ice Storm   20
Iceman Discovered By a German Couple   22
After Innisfree   24
Spawning the Space   26
Ache   27
Paris Light: November   28
Curve   29
Evolutionary   30
Dwelling   31

II: LIGHT

Words   35
Singing   36
Night Light   38
Perception   39
Heidegger's *Gelassenheit*   40
Wouldn't It Be Better   41
Entropy   42
The Distance   43
Momentary   45
Cruel Radiance   46
Need   48
Mind   50
Windows   51
Appeal   52

III: FAMILY

My Grandmother's Name   55
Lineage   56
The Photograph   57
Leaving the World   59
Before I Was Born   61
Disappearance   62
This Picture   64
What Is and What Is Not   67
Gift   68
Press   69

What's a Memory   70
A Late Apology   72
Instead   74
Childhood   75
That I May Understand   76
Remembering a Husband   78
Sense   79
Grandmothers   80

IV: ART

Tableau   83
At The Museum Of Natural History:
    Reading Leonardo Da Vinci's Codex   84
Still Life with Music   87
The Dance   88
Schumann's Opus 21: Three Voices   89
Shapes Dissolves Into Color   92
Frida Kahlo Thinks Of Death   94
Millais' Painting: *Ophelia*   95
Chest Pains: Weymouth Center for the Arts   97
Sexton   99
Reading *Outer Dark*   100
Uncertain   101
After Paula's Death Clara Westhoff Speaks   103
Kathe Kollwitz Sketches Her Son   105
Intimations   106
We Stand Before Van Gogh's Last Painting   107
Exhibit of Van Gogh in Blues and Greens   108

Ancestors   *109*
Conversation at the Edge   *110*
Meditation   *112*

PART V: ENDINGS

Survivor   *115*
Finishing Touches   *116*
Confession   *118*
Arcadian   *119*
The Past   *120*
"So We Live Here, Forever Taking Leave"   *122*
Holding   *123*
Lives They Left Behind   *124*
Memory of a Student's Untimely Death   *125*
Pavane   *126*
Promise   *127*
That Kingdom   *129*
After The Death Camps   *131*
Earth Borne   *132*
A Runner's Quarrel   *133*
Timanfaya Lava Fields: Canary Islands   *135*
The Apple   *136*
What Is Found   *137*

Afterword   *139*
Acknowledgments   *141*

Foreword

What is the word I want, I ask myself, to describe the unique quality I find in each of the poems by Annette Allen? What is it that she does in poem after poem that both amazes and satisfies me?

Lying in bed in the dark and the quiet, body at ease, and mind at rest alone with itself, I find myself wanting the simple and true word, a sort of key that unlocks the treasure chest of her achievement, poem after poem.

> And I find it.
> Each poem is a gathering.
> They are gatherings.
> [Later, I will think "gatherings like a granary."]

Each poem embraces complexity, and through memory and abstraction, past and present, through comparison and contrast, through perceiving how each moment is inhabited by complexity—both what it is and what it is not—there is not mere reconciliation but celebration—the celebration of what is.

In what is, Annette Allen gives us both what was, (AND, here's the miracle:) and what ever shall be.

Why? And how?

The answer to both questions is the same: in her work, she has unified craft and intuition, intellect and emotion, call and response, and the result is the creation of art. Art that partakes of the eternal.

The mastery of, the achieve of, (as Gerard Manley Hopkins writes in his poem "The Windhover") the thing I'm calling ART. In poem after poem, her poems, the artifact of the poem rides the air. It holds us miraculously aloft in the moment. It defies the forces that would bring us down and leave us shattered. She shows us how to soar above individual pain and gigantic atrocity.

One may need to read these poems more than once. So what? They stand there, sculptures of the airy word, beautiful and replete with meaning, lighted from within, waiting for thee.

Sena Jeter Naslund
Author of *Ahab's Wife*, *Four Spirits*,
and *The Fountain of St. James Court,
or Portrait of the Artist as an Old Woman*

For in the immediate world, everything is to be discerned, for him who can discern it, and centrally and simply, without either dissection into science, or digestion into art, but with the whole of consciousness, seeking to perceive it as it stands: so that the aspect of a street in sunlight can roar in the heart of itself as a symphony, perhaps as no symphony can: and all of consciousness is shifted from the imagined, the revisive, to the effort to perceive the cruel radiance of what is.

James Agee
Let Us Now Praise Famous Men

To look life in the face, always to look life in the face, and to know it for what it is, at last . . . to love it for what it is, and then to put it away.

Virginia Woolf
To The Lighthouse

for Osborne Wiggins
Philosopher of Infinite Tasks

I
Place

> Lost in thickets, houses flicker messages
> from lives within. My memory decodes them.
> This landscape so familiar stings with beauty.
> — "Late"

Late

Finding my way to you through fields of stars,
down roads, muscled into earth, loosened by rain,
I think of the country of my Iowa childhood.
Night throws her hand over these worn barns,
their planks sprung and patched with tin.
Lost in thickets, houses flicker messages
from lives within. My memory decodes them.
This landscape so familiar stings with beauty.

Even you, steady in your singing between strings,
on wood chambered and echoing, even the stove
you stoke with split wood, the old 78 records
you play, 12th Street Rag and the Ink Spots:
all summon rhythms of ache and refrain.
Here close to earth in a hermit's stone house
you live surrounded by trees, everything
elemental: sky, land, water, fire, basic as bone.

What does it mean to have come here so late,
to be pulled by time to this rudimentary place?
Will this world you tend like a young plant
open and flower as all my remembering has?
Too late to turn back, I slip on your clothes,
watch how you nurture thought, the cat, me.
I wrap myself in your sleeping bag, your care.
You bank the fire. All night I sleep in its glow.

Beverly Drive

This must be the street, named
as it is for an unknown girl.
I should have recognized it,
known it would come to this.
Always a closed-off road, once
wild with magnolia and pecan,
outspread trees guiding children
and graveled driveways
over sloping stretches,
now overbuilt. Houses loom
the paved paths, precise lawns.

The heart calls
sun, December sun,
come out, give me more light,
lead me past fenced yards
and dry leaves. Call back
the old road, unfolding
a bright scarf of memory,
afternoons ample with green,
voices silken, murmuring
names, blue sound of the train
streaking the fabric.

Light it up slowly,
touching each purple iris,
stalk of hollyhock, ivy

scrambling the walk, lift
from the shadows two
small boys chasing a dog,
and settle at last on the spot
of the fig tree now gone,
its leaves once large enough
to cover me, as they did
Eve after the Fall.

Between Piano and Door

Stepping to the horizon of childhood
streets where Earl's Grocery
has been erased and karaoke bars
replace the local Feed and Supply Store
on South Main, I mine long gone,
unbound fields, open the buried
passages, crying I've come back.

A table set with white blossoms,
flow-blue plates brimming
with berries, and you are here,
blind, growing shorter the older
you get, bent like the fingers you spread
over keys playing Schumann's *Traumerei*.

The song floats a bright shape
through silence to your husband
of sixty-two years preparing pie,
unable to hear the music. He still drives
the '78 Mercury, tells me to give
everyone the right of way.

Each note colors the lilac
scented air with the past,
how he used to lift his head
from his task, hum along,
then walk across the threshold
to touch your dress.

I have always known this,
the sharps and flats, the steps,
more or less, between piano and door
open for stars and the waiting dark.
Here lights are burning down like
candles, while across town the house
where I lived is no longer there.

Stillness

As a child, you watched
your mother slip into another world,
as if becalmed on water
the color of transfixed eyes.
At sea in an ocean of detail,
she never knew where to look,
desire circled, spun like driftwood.

In the freedom to not move,
not see what others did,
perhaps she held sadness back
or silence shut out clamor
from the past: the love she buried
under a gray stone slab, chickens
roaming her husband's dying farm.
In the field an overturned hoe.

Your mother's hush said "Be Still"
to the plea of anyone's needs.
No questions, no five-year-old wants.
Like a bride she waited,
each separate calm
prelude to certain rescue.
While you, still mute, knew
the one she waited for
would not appear.

You've grown familiar with shades
of stillness, the power to define
what surrounds it, to mark the in-between.
Beyond devotion and dread,
memory of her is stored away,
a varnished, sacred painting.
There she's entranced,
a Madonna haloed by light
you could never comprehend.

Portrait

You would never overlook her.
All that quiet seduces your glance
smoother than the enchantments
of her skin that might yield
like cream to tongue's touch,
or light the dark around the body
as the flesh of twelfth-century monks
illuminated the books they read.

Her other self, caught beneath paint,
holds within its tangle, a girl
cradled as if by roots of a tree,
breathing cautiously, trying to slow
the heat toward womanhood,
and in the higher branches
like a luminous balloon,
there is the moon, her face.

She knows someone watches.
Her lower lip wary, bruised by
beauty, closes. The black eyes focus,
cells of darkness reaching out
to seize your breath and hold it,
intent on an intruder whose
irrevocable words are still held back
like an arrow in a long-drawn bow.

Phone Call at the MacDowell Colony

It begins with the voice
    on the phone miles away
speaking as if under water,
    telling of a current problem,
another crisis,
    or why would I think
of a sea cucumber so far inland,
    how it divides its flesh in two
whenever in danger,
    the middle of the body tears open,
splits into two selves,
    and it offers one self,
succulent plant of that world,
    to be engulfed,
perhaps devoured,
    making a self-section, a chasm,
so the other self can edge away
    in a broken whisper,
to write this poem, salvaging
    ripped boundaries, saying yes
to the lesson in survival.

Staying On

Each day the Chicago heat searing
the garden's wildness helps you
look for him. The foliage he once
planted, almost a thicket now,
opens the memory you water
at dusk. Like a wary farmer,
you prepare for possible drought.

In the wilted housedress, you
surrender to hunger, grief,
as Russian women might at market,
offering tomatoes and lean corn,
their fingers like yours grown raw
rubbing against stems, leaves.

These summer months burn on,
like distant lights where cars
stop and go, their riders wedged
between birth and death. Still
staying on, you haul the hose to
each fern, blossom, bittersweet vine,
then touch the aged twin willow
that shadows the sun spotted yard.

Your hand pulls to the place
where the trunk divides.
The tree's bark, warm and dry
from heat, recalls the way fire
makes wood sing, as if the sealed-
in song of one lone nightingale
still lived in the tree.

Severing Old Beliefs

In Africa, sleeping in the tropics
seemed exotic under the mosquito net,
cotton cloud dropping from a canopy
any princess would want, its frayed
hemp edge caught in the bedding.

A gossamer world blurred frangepani
blossoms outside, outlines lost
in the faultless sky. So nothing's clear
in this tucked-in memory but the rub
of sheet as today's paper tells me,

Malaria Makes a Comeback.

How impossible to live that vanished life,
somehow invented, tangled in ignorance.
Instead, the newspaper brings back fever,
late night-sweats that leave me shaky, like
a small boy on buckling ground who could

die in fifteen seconds. Now it's "common
as a scraped knee," losing a child to malaria;
before you can cook plantain, the fire
sputters out. Sympathy hangs in the air
like flies or mosquitoes who visit the poor.

It's More Deadly Than Before.

Banana trees still dot the hillside
of viridian green, where, for five dollars,
I know sleepers could dream under
that vital net, sucking for breath,
shedding weight of probable death.

It's a worn-out rope that ties me to
a fanciful past, no diaphanous string,
I drag the mind's floor, wishing
for shells. Only to sever old beliefs
on the coral reef of headlines.

The Dark Continent

for Carol Gilligan

> *I bring you the plague.*
> —*Sigmund Freud*

You are first to penetrate the unspoiled land,
Dr. Freud, as you travel this silent river back
to its source. Later you tell the analysand

how you remember trees, their black
limbs hanging the heavy curtain
that closed behind you. No almanac

could chronicle the moon changes when
none but you would dare this void. You call
it the dark world of women's sex, then

reaching for entry find yourself in thrall
to the interior air where night jars displace
stillness. At dawn you watch the river's dull

surface for clues to this natal place,
see familiar flesh shaped with your past
life. It mirrors back a man's face.

Long you explore this continent cast
in your shadow, inscribe a virginal map
marking dangers, wild weeds that last

in a pristine land. Strange maladies wrap
you in fire and a sign of plague appears.
Yet you chant your magic hoping to trap

the unnameable. After you spend years
telling of this, your mouth closes slowly
over the fever still blistering there.

Die Vermissten
1939-1945

Monument outside Schwandorf, Germany

A gray monument engraves
the city's peril, strained words:
Die Vermissten: the missing.

Blood-red leaves drift alongside,
downstream beyond Schwandorf
or drop, a sudden forest fall
that catches the breath.

Villagers still wait for a sign,
wait to drape a coffin in black,
to stammer through last words,
or glorify return of the prodigal.

Where have you gone
these seventy years,
after you hurled a rifle
into underbrush or filthy trench,
turned from the wounded,
gaping holes of flesh.

Were you startled
into the ground, camouflaged
like a field animal, invisible in snow.
A white ribcage some creature
once had a heart in.

*O missing ones,
friend, son, or lover,
where are you now?
where did you go,
what did you want?*

Carve a stone for us
that still offers hope, you said,
one that chronicles absence,
claims the lost.
Write us down,
name names.

German Cities

Schwandorf, a stage-set village:
Medieval church, reconstructed steeple,
near a mill's turning wooden wheel,
its thatched covered bridge still
reaches across the stream;
all rebuilt as life before the war.
In traditional dress women bustle
into the square, actors on cue,
friendly, red-armed, flowers in hand.

Nuremberg's not far away.
Home of Riesenstahl's staged parade
where Hitler mesmerized massive
Nazi rallies, in footage of martial
jackboot clicks, the famous *Heil*.
Now the ground shakes to the beat
of rock concerts on another stage
set over dusty grass and slabs,
but it's empty most days.

Both cities invite attention,
possible affection, after
the Third Reich's theatrics:
seductive appearance of power
or quaint restored charm.
Two kinds of artifice—
some would say, art—
spun from realities
we try to understand
and even bear.

After the Ice Storm

> *It was one of those places where that*
> *magnificent peacock we call nature*
> *seems to strut before our eyes*
>   —*Victor Hugo*

Viewing the Rhine, Hugo knew
the true eye of earth is water, a flowing
form that gives us back the self
hovering beneath a divided surface
of rivers, lakes. Here in the sand hills,
the eye opens to an overnight world,
which shines, intimate, the crystal
branches letting down their hair
in strands of water that mirror sky.

Whatever falls today mesmerizes,
a slice of liquid streaming into the cup,
breath's frosted steam, even magnolia
leaves shattering like glass. Everything
that makes us see, sees, as morning baptizes
this last known stand of longleaf pine,
the drops pooling for the red cockaded
woodpecker, almost extinct, still
living in cavities of old-growth trees.

Listen. If the birds are telling of it,
back and forth through the damp
streets of air, over the ice-glazed

thickets, it's not about the sunlight
ricocheting off the pond's eye where
birds drink, but that water remains
distinct after drinking, its skin intact,
and somehow they know they will
come and go, but water outlasts them.

"Iceman Discovered by a German Couple"

(headline in an American newspaper)

I

Once a hairy-bodied man who unset traps,
who ran with beasts without thinking
and captured a woman who became the door
to the house of the dead, he sits without shelter.

They found him in the Tyrolean Alps,
his head lifted to wintering light,
dreams shimmering on his lips, frostbite tight,
silenced by profound dehydration.

A skeleton well-preserved in traumatic
blows, fractured ribs, hairline breaks
in bones, even evidence of arthritic calcification.
An arrowhead lodges in his chest cage.

Similar to modern humans in health conditions,
scientists claim, flashing tomographic images,
carbon dating the body back five thousand years,
older than the mummy of Tutankhamun.

II

I wonder what my bones would reveal
in a thousand years, having smashed
my chest on a bike's handlebars yesterday,

and sure that I've fractured my sternum
to match the cracked clavicle, broken ribs
in the past. Just think: an unexpected collision,
momentary darkness in the skull's room
of earth's pulsing green would fragment

my breath, and leave only the instant before death.
But my bones, calcified, splintered, without
wound read years later will trumpet in gesture
a wild song of having lived, if only by chance.

After Innisfree

Remember how the island looked,
those first days after marriage,
lifting its luminous trees and earth
from the lake's gray sheet,
the image wavering in dusk and
wish that it be what Yeats claimed:
idyllic, mysterious as the bright
currents shifting around us.

Didn't the water seem to love
the forest stretched across its body,
and the trees adore that embrace?
Wasn't the sky doubled within us
as well, its color tender, truer than
the real? Like dreamers, whatever
we found in that moment slept on
our eyelids, passed through hands.

Years later we think of that trip,
how we walked into forest shadows
one day where an old man dressed
in a suit and vest surfaced from green
shamrocked slopes. Barely upright,
yet smiling, a walking stick oaring
him on, we say he is the charm,
an elf in our story. Perhaps.

Though he could be a diviner instead,
his faltering breath and step
hint of our own descent from Innisfree:
bodies incandescent with desire,
surprised by roots and steep fall
of land underfoot but still carrying
that after-image of light and bearing
an ache in the side before darkness.

Spawning the Space

If language were as crystalline
as its promise seems to suggest,
if it were that clear breath
of sense to reveal reality,
to give each object's soul
flight in winds
of pure meaning,

then this river of pale
strands wavering in blue
shallows along the shore,
like a woman on her knees,
sunlit hair thrown forward
over lily pad and primal reeds,
might bring nature's body

to speech,
that haunting lyric,
spawning the space between
this moment and the next,
without borders, without
limits or perpetual hunger
for completion.

Ache

Can it be that longing
causes the brilliant orange-red
of these leaves and compels
the branch's stretch for autumn
sun? Or is it the wish to be
consumed that blazes this fire
through the trees lining the street,
in a direction so unmistakable,
I must not look long?

Is desire a color that flames out
at death, regretting nothing, not
even abandonment? Or is it
a constant ache to move easily
against the evening sky, ready
at last to caress the earth's body,
a desire so insistent in its grief,
it can turn any green leaf, as if by
divine disturbance, to a glorious red?

Paris Light: November

In this country that does not celebrate
Thanksgiving, it is a thanksgiving
morning when the sun's flaming fingers
bless leafless, tapered trees
and sienna tiled roofs.

Here, years earlier, light haloed the hair
of cathedral travelers caught
in transition between illuminations.
In another November, Monet had
remembered the shadow of war

with flowers gathered in such light,
and this same brightening landscape
struck Pissarro, his brush blurring
the edges, stroking the bushes to fire.
All this happened long ago, before

the City of Light opened its borders,
welcomed the Eagles of Death Metal Band
to Theatre Bataclan, years before
terrorists twisted that November light
into the blood of the European storm.

Yet everywhere today, over market stalls
of lettuce and fruit, pungent cheeses,
and bristling roosters in cages, gold
and orange spill a light still more
miraculous than sacramental wine.

Curve

The way evening comes to the silver birch
bending toward the field, each branch almost
lost in smoke-gray, recalls the moment
before dawn curves over the slope of land,
spreading the violet of the sky beginning.

I could wish for little more than the curve
of late-winter sky or the field's turn beyond
my vision. Perhaps the pattern that replays
curve, the shape of the world, in apples
and flushed nipples, a tiny ear that turns

back on itself, the arc of spray dashed
against the rocks, even the open face
of the moon, is the same one that pulls me
to the bend of an arm, the force that turns
all things, circling around in full caress.

Evolutionary

Each time we walk the beach,
the ancient reach of seas pulls
at shoes. Our blood knows this salt,
these primal cells, even lime still
lodges in the bones.
                        Shirts fly off

our backs, socks are disowned
while we scavenge in seaweed
and drifted wood, like refugees
returning home
                        after three billion years.

Other creatures vanished, leaving
the edge of a tiger's tooth, a veined
stain. But we, with our human brain
dream-seamed and hungry, still burn
by power of the leaf,
                        a plant's green

breath harnessing light from a sun.
Across time we bear earth's memory
before our birth and touch through
sidereal space a world
                        our flesh will not enter.

Dwelling

> *Dwelling is the manner in which*
> *mortals are on earth.*
> *—Martin Heidegger*

Each day we lean into the earth
flying its endless orbit
where everything is just
beyond our reach and say:

Become the wind, the mist and rain,
soak the tree's root and gather
what light remains into this windowed
world, these numinous hours.

There is nothing to fear
in this land of sunlight,
not even a heart scraped bare,
there's only sky's beckoning blue.

II
Light

the shell's lace unfolded,
as it turned in the light,
the lettering inscrutable
and innocent as stars are,
of any human need
for meaning.
—"Need"

Words,

such small shapes, capture
        the world's blooming
like wildflowers, a cup of light,

or use reason's rope to prove
        what lies beyond them.
Human made, they darken

over years as old paintings do,
        the way varnish on a portrait
deepens the speaking face

or sometimes

as the heart swings
        back and forth in the body—
a bell ringing its joy—

words celebrate the sky,
        altar of shared dreams
and morning sun.

Singing

in pairs, the nuns process
under the monastery dome,
their cloistered voices
ascending beyond those
still rooted in this world.

Gray heads nodding,
their backs stooped,
fragile arms hanging,
they look ordinary
in loose, colorless clothes,
like any group of old women.

But they move toward the infinite,
not tempted like others
to shake back the surge of years:
to touch up a tracery of lines,
find the husband buried a decade before,
or call a cab back to the dance
they left one night.

This music claims them,
raptures them into a larger lyric.
Women who once could swim and run,
live in the hope that angels
in stained glass hear their notes,
unmindful of what
frail bodies fall to.

I will remember the ache
of seeing them, how I wanted
to dress each in liturgical robes,
habits of the past,
shroud them in dark dignity,
soft folds hiding bent shoulders,
old bones.

Someday the sisters will leave
their names to echo
in church rolls of the dead.
Yet in my mind they rise,
black reeds vibrant with melody,
making a cathedral
of the ground.

Night Light

Waking these nights in this cave
of a room is to see shadows
roam wallpapered walls, cross
the uneven wood floor, its paint
scraped thin in places by other
writers who walked, trying on words,
like ear muffs, gloves, against
possible chill or failure. What am I
doing with a flickering night-light
at this age, tracing in half-tones
my smoky life that burns back in
the mind somewhere, some space,
and opens in the darkness,
spreading restless wings.

Lying in this small bed, I'm a child
charmed by a Proustian lantern,
its magic of dark and day; delivered
at last from all that's actual:
the cumbersome weight of dishes,
letters from home, even my solid
body, everything factual, limited.
Instead of trying to sleep
at this unearthly hour, freighted
with probable burdens, promise
of work, I enter where all things
began, the summer of childhood,
transfigured with images of flight
this time, outside history and regret.

Perception

At first, the sensible is
only a vague beckoning,
that song of color
at eye's edge,
calling the earth into view.
Then spring ripens its fruit,
coaxes me to follow,
and where land was once—
grass, woods, ground—
cornflowers unfold
their blue, a lifting sea,
summoning the senses,
each wave's whisper,
scent of salt,
my flesh echoing all:
azure petal and shape,
this world's lullaby,
rocking the breathing
body into dance.

Heidegger's Gelassenheit*

Here leaves rustle sounds without a why,
the flowing current forms a space disclosing
time, a letting be. Receptive and adrift, this quiet
erases demand, the will to will what happens.

To air instead the lightening that opens
silence, charges cold boundaries of stones
surrounding the heart; the self, now less
insistent on some consoling truth, prepares to fly.

Uncharted now, covenants unravel like
clouds streaming the sky. I forget old songs
learned in school. A stranger to myself,
I know a green world's already come.

* *releasement*

Wouldn't it Be Better

The grave danger is tears
when you look back,
distance preserves the sea,
its immeasurable miles
where nothing is simply one thing:
the bottle floating,
boat overturned, spilling lives
like stones on a beach you walk,
regretting what is abandoned.

Compelled to look back,
you might not see autumn trees
unwrap their gold coin.
Or hear the rise and swell of strings
in Bach's Double Concerto
flowing toward you and back,
or even relish the kiss
that promises what you touch
becomes you at last.

The glance backward brings
unstoppable tears, not in the wilderness
of bodies or the mysteries of humankind.
It offers contemplation that absorbs all.
Wouldn't it be better to steal
the clear radiance at dusk,
and believe in that moment
you could go on a little longer
before the sun drops.

Entropy

Night stares back, a face
through a passing car window,
stars sprinkle the darkness,
a cold breath
expanding the lung of space.
Constellations cast
an illusion of permanence.

Human love is more steadfast
than an accident of physics.
Daily we shake out our clothes
for the comforting chatter
of static in the material
of this human life,
its brief shine.

Some day our star will collapse,
each creature, every leaf
folded in its arms. Our love
will not be different in its
ending. When a star
succumbs to exhaustion,
its ribbon threads the sky.

The Distance

Consciousness begins with distance,
they say, even the newborn stunned
by separateness wails the ancient claim
for home, oneness. Beyond the boundary
of his small body, the universe spins away.

This is how the age-long reach begins,
that same groping of the past billion years,
cells bringing the sea ashore, tracing
its salty embrace in a curved foot,
life beating on, desire knocking

in the veins. Even the mammoths
must have trumpeted grief, traveling
the immense distance, ready to find
home before they laid down their bones
and centuries turned them to stone.

What can I tell you of such anguished
yearning or the heart's restless passage
from grassland to rarified air, like a hawk
finding its mate in a wing-dance of cries,
not content to live in the distance.

For a long time things happen in the earth
we can't see, the way love can begin in
a dying season, or even the past; then,

like the glorious reach of cornstalk for sky,
we find miles and years collapsed.
And once in a lifetime, if we are lucky
on a trail of yellow pine and algaed stone,
we may merge with sunlight, air and water
while eons of forming hills and deserts pass,
and the mind moves back to its beginnings.

Momentary

Perhaps it's the color, pristine
white, that invites me to lie down,
to shed the world like a coat, dull
wrapping I have worn these years.
Or it's silence speaking in branch-
burdened truths, echoing slow
collapse over layered ground.

This snow washes my mind
with solitude's stroke, transforms
what we call sleet to a curtain of
descending light. I stand here
under the edged splinters of light
which have gone out or exploded

into the universe. They're more certain
of destiny than I am. Like gauze covering
everything scarred, the tree we carve
names in or some snapped weeds,
snow drifts a momentary bandage, its salve
of wonder and caution of white over
what we know, did not or could not last.

Cruel Radiance

(for my parents)

Tonight light touches
a woman's forehead
as she lifts her head to sing,
a man's hand
as he cradles his violin.

Arranged as they are
in this half-light,
banked in dusky green,
they suggest a pastoral painting.
Somewhere the grass is mowed.

I don't know where,
but the scent intensifies
everything
about these two caught
on the edge of song.

If the man shudders
from the cut-grass
smell of damp and rot
or from the breath
of night just beyond

the hills, or whether
they intend to stay long
or only a moment
before they begin to blur,
I can't say.

I can tell you there is tenderness
in the line of their bodies,
fatigue in his,
and that around them
the cruel, radiant light still dances.

Need

The Eskimo knows
the soul of the universe
is never seen, though
its voice may be heard
sometimes in the dance
of storm or nocturnal fire.
I thought I glimpsed it
once in the breakers' toss
of an alphabet shell
imprinted with golden
characters circling its cone.
Like Darwin in the Galapagos
reading beaks of finches,
or a shaman eyeing cracks
of the bear's shoulder bone,
I lifted from the sea's green
the message hungered for.

Almost a hieroglyph,
the shell's lace unfolded
as it turned in the light,
the lettering inscrutable
and innocent, as stars are,
of any human need
for meaning.
I search each landscape,

the shades of snowfall
or wrinkles in night sky,
to decipher
the world's body,
its elusive map.
Even the flight of birds
a writing to be read.

Mind

No one can claim with certainty
her own mind, certainly not like
fingertips nor the beating heart,
whose passion wells then dissembles
as it passes: a momentary wave
chasing after the real, that original
touch which made it tremble.

But beyond this body-to-body
world of coded cells and tissue,
there is another, hooded in bone,
yet distant, an interior zone we
make far from the green expanse
of woods; a space for flight
and drifting like a bird in possibility.

We might call it an open archway
to a country of light still haunted by
the night that will extinguish it.
Limitless, the light streams, undone
briefly by an old poem, veiled griefs;
its long rays reaching islands, ideas
and dreams where there are none.

Windows

Remember how you slept in a glass-lined room
in our first house, how each morning the windows
struck your heart with light, and you woke,
climbing two steps to find us, as if to another life.

Now boards cover the windows that entranced,
shutter the memory of love's claim and need.
You wear time's suit like armor, a ready
reflex against damage, and I remember what

was promised: that like fate, the family
continues forever. Perhaps the loss is finally
about what never was and pain's a feverish cure,
like fire burning the forest to new green.

Yet something hinders healing; as in beginning
speech, words cannot be found. You look out
the window into the dark where the stars
survive like syllables of a lost language.

Appeal

Isn't there something in us that
hungers for fierce transcendence,
some pagan holdover that delivered
nature to life by creating gods:
god of the wind, Aoelus, and
Triton, old ruler of the sea?

Yearning for nature's purity
is suspect now. There's not much
place for ideals written over the real.
Human gesture—intimate and erotic—
enrapts us. The world is legible on the skin,
grounding each domestic bliss.

Yet mixed with this—the appeal
to hold another's face to lips, eyes—
isn't there a residue of desire
to be the rain as it touches down,
to feel the shape that love
takes for all creation.

For the way morning cracks
along ancient river beds and a mist
lifts off the trembling trees, those tall
green steeples, wind loosening
their tongues until the air rings
the world into an awakening hue.

III

Family

> I remember how wide the future was
> when it was all imagination: a slate blue
> lake that matched the climbing sky.
> I know we can touch it with our hands.
> — "Instead"

My Grandmother's Name

Iowa summer sun whitewashes the birch
rising above my grandmother's grave, woman
I never knew, nine months dead when I was born.
It scorches the turf as it turns toward her husband,
blistered by typhoid she could not heal, though
his blood lived on in four daughters. Underground,
my grandparents' roots twist tightly together, and
as a child, wild sounds of love lifted to me.

Don't believe that old story about children,
how they fail to think of sex between parents.
Singed grass traced the passion between them,
the world and its cravings not gone for those lying
down before their time. The imagination is dark
and starry. Like a constellation, it has its own logic,
no link lies between what is and what I saw. Except
my tiny-boned grandmother, hair down to her

waist working the corn fields, one day walked away
to marry a man named Strange who was exactly that.
He lifted her up with an uncanny song that still
haunts the hearts in this place, and now mine. Under
this blazing sun, I can imagine difficulties of the world
burned away and love desperate enough to step from
a calm bed to the skin of another life. I read the name
on my grandmother's tombstone again. It is my own.

Lineage

I do not remember my father playing the violin,
nor the way his frail body bent toward the sound,
a Picasso stroke in the lift of his shoulder and arm,
each note gracing his blue eyes that focus beyond
the budding Iowa spring that will outlive him.

I do not remember my grandmother shawled
in black, shades drawn as she paged her bible,
pressing four-leaf clovers between the lips
of God, her voice, a thread of light in the dark,
singing, "We are going home. To die no more."

So I have no memory that explains this seduction
to music I have not heard. No image from the past
to flesh out or erase. Yet a descending line connects
my heartbeat to the fugue of death, a touch cast
through time, searing this found book and a violin.

The Photograph

(for my father)

This is a still life,
a brown study of six men,
motionless in white shirts.
One is much younger than
the others as they stand
single file, arms crossed,
a company of workers
flanked by a barber pole.
It is June between the wars
when you come to a standstill,
fixed at eighteen forever.
Only in this place are you
constant, faithful in your gaze
across the years lost to me.

When I finally learned
there were fathers,
my mother unearthed your
graven face, handed me this
memento mori to carry
all my life. Death was nothing
to me then. I waited for you.
Together we would escape
this sad woman listening
to Rimsky-Korsakov each night.
Your eyes would be blue,

not brown, your hair like mine.
Grown now I still long to say:
Listen, it only takes a moment
to begin, to live the life you
have become. But nothing
moves on this drab summer day.
Behind you, store front windows
extend inward, their dusty
shine encasing your body.
No sign of change to come.
Only these words scrawled
across the picture's back:
"I am dropping you a card
from the shop I work in.
See if you can find me."

Leaving the World

When father died
you lost the milk to feed me.
Two days you sat in
St. Joseph Mercy Hospital,
hand on empty breast,
saying this is not mercy,
not this. Already
you were beginning to leave me,
bearing your body and his
to Gracewood Cemetery.

The stones called you to death.
Like priests they blessed
your solemn journey,
marking the way of the ancients,
mother and father before you,
they consecrated the ground.
The green grave accepted you both,
him once and you day after day,
the grass drying
to the shape of your barren body.

Each year I made supplication,
placing flowers you gathered
on Memorial Day,
praising my father, secretly entreating
him to give you back,

please, father.
I will make a sacrifice.
Still you moved farther away.
Halfway through a meal
your blue eyes would stare nowhere.

Carrying the book of progress,
you left this world,
making pilgrimage down
the path cut in your soul.
In time you were no longer there.
Never having had you
I cannot let you go,
nor can I be delivered.
I look into the stare of any
stranger to find you.

Before I Was Born

You must have turned to him,
your eyes slowed by the October sky
halfway to winter,
your quickening body
shadowing his, curving with life
before the window light.

My father must have wanted you then,
all the way back to the early years
when long hair swept your face
at each turn of a swing. He must have
said so, stretched his failing frame
toward life, his hunger for your breasts
deep as mine would be the next day.

In your arms you rocked him backward
past the moment I was conceived, plunged
back to your own birth, the hour
when you first learned the language
of the body, each touch changing you
from newborn to lover and back again
in the place where beginning is end.

The moment enfolded you, held you both
on course with a cord that measured
his life in six months. Yet you would
live another twenty years, mother,
and I, I still have not surfaced in this life.
My birth and his death pulled us
forever out of the womb.

Disappearance

I try to imagine how it happened:
      the slight shift of your foot on
the gangplank, then the arm flung out
      like a seagull's wing
to steady your body, bending,
      almost folding into the dive
you made time and again
      as a boy at Leif Erickson Pool,
but this time striking the anchored ship,
      breaking the current's mirror,
the circles spreading forward to me
      watching my own image
sharpen in the waves.

This is what I do to understand
      hunger for the harbor's mouth,
for the plunge to haul a brother's broken body-
      my arms now older, stronger-
to the top: I remember
      your visits home,
how I would hug an unfamiliar smell:
      you tossing me up, catching
me back, joys rare to the widowed
      world of our mother.
You would appear, a soft light
      of winter subverting gray,
then like a god, disappear.

Nothing happens once and ends
        scenes flow toward us and back:
visions of a downward flight,
        memory of a last good-bye,
the requested kiss, never-given,
        withheld, with me
at the edge of shyness and puberty,
        not knowing that
the present can't be forever.
        Let sadness swell the sea,
spill you once more,
        on shore for that last embrace
before you disappear again.

This Picture

I
Photograph of Two Sisters: *Summer*

In a meadow outside this picture, childhood
lives with Queen Anne's Lace and Goldenrod
growing in riotous run for sunlight.

Imagine upturned faces flushed by heat-
glazed sky where blue-eyed sisters act out
stories. We wear weeds as crowns on our

white hair, though you're the queen and
I'm your fair lady-in-waiting. In the distance
someone's thresher thrums, splitting seeds

from husk, each breath repeating the past
one. I watch wheat bend and you stand,
a separate gold leaf. Soon swallows will

sweep you closer to the green cover of grass.
For years, the birds cry across the fields
and so do I: *come back, I still wait for you.*

II
The House on Grandview Street: *Autumn*

Come back, I still wait for you,
for the swallows to bring garlands

left in a dry, turned field, for your
quick step on stairs in the house
that didn't have a grand view or a
mother. Say I never sat in that chair,

towel around my neck while blonde
strands of hair fell like leaves
outdoors. Never screamed when

you cut off the tip of my ear, leaving
a hollow, the mark I bear, totem
I touch when I can't find words.

III
St. Joseph's Mercy Hospital: *Winter*

I touch when I can't find words,
hoping you will hear me through
the skin, translucent now, like
the flesh of Renoir's women

who bear his mark standing at the piano
or window, faces soft with satisfaction,
round bodies rosy in spots, greenish-white
mostly, like flesh that's been dead for days.

Something about your spare winter
room reminds me of green garlands
at Christmas, the surprise of ice skates,
how you hid them until I said *Mercy,*
each day I will wait for you by the skate rink
frozen like the ice in milk you drink for pain,
or your body in its last gesture; blue eyes
vacant as a stripped bed the following day.

IV

East State Street: *Spring*

A stripped bed the following day
should be planted with care, the priest
tells me, referring to the garden

I touch when I can't find words,
but he means my life, this breath
repeating the past, wanting Goldenrod

and weeds to weave into garlands,
though not for hair. I wait for
spring's heartbeat under that

green cover of grass. *Am I still*
a sister, I cry to flying swallows
in a meadow outside this picture.

What Is and What Is Not

At dusk when houses forgot their doors,
and farmers went hatless, my sister pulled
me barefoot under shady oak, past
the drugstore of vanilla cokes where yellow
suns fringed the path to the bandshell.

Music opened its wings to the wind who
lifted a baton, a signal for fireflies to
flicker, the small fires kissing the grass,
lighting sharps and notes of the band's tune
straining for crescendo at evening's end.

Each blade of fire was overture to reverie,
that song of playful solitude where
what is and what is not fuse in flame,
changeable and fugitive as love would be.
On Sunday nights at the concerts,

the tiny torches banished darkness,
like lighted candles that say you are
on holy ground, or like this memory
in its pleasure, knowing fire smolders
in ash and surely in the soul.

Gift

You hold me to this life
as surely as I carried you
all winter under my heart,
that perishable organ
which opens and closes.
Each time I want to close
my eyes in that last sleep,
your pulse opens in mine,
charges the field of my body,
its rivers of bone.
The morning you were born
Aprils ago, your face
bore witness to the pain
and flowering of this world.
I now know
whatever we live by
leads back
to such clear beginnings.

Press

When he was young
my son showed me
a fossil unearthed
in our back yard:
the small stone
imprinted, gray engraving,
a pattern perfected inside.

In Hiroshima after
the bomb descended,
I've learned
there were shadow pictures
of people burned
into the ground
by the blast.

Each morning now
we turn in bed,
hold our bodies hard
together, your chest
etching my breast
the press of parting
rolling over us.

What's a Memory?

> *Something from long ago, my lad.*
> *—a child's story*

As far back as the thirteenth century
our memory stretches, back into layers
of black basalt and volcanic tuff,

past rain and wind carving the cliffs
we climb, your eight year-old body
in search of other worlds. The air

thin, we blur through backdrop of sky
to Anasazi fires, where long ago
an old tale flamed the tongue, where

now dust circles the Puye ruins.
We have come here to remember
something essential, something

lost in a world with sidewalks, though
you don't know that. We want to leave
signs of our faithfulness in the storm

circles, frog figures inscribing season's
ritual in rock. This moment brims with
how lives go on across time; how ashes

and worn tools collect in the midden;
and how Native Americans believe all things
must be returned to earth. Though I want to,

I don't say we hand on whatever we can,
and that someday I will leave you still
searching for shards, fragments, stories.

A Late Apology

(for my son, Montaigne)

You never liked it, the name we chose
for you, sifted from the coals of learning.
It flames at me from the road sign
near Bordeaux, the signal of what remains
of Montaigne's chateau and his greatness:
a tower, the fearless question,

Que sais je? What do I know?

I ask it now: *What do I know?*

That truth layers the air I breathe.
Its smoke colors the trees grey behind me,
unfurls the path I pedal, remembering
your first-grade face, the failure of trust
when the teacher attempted your name.

The French call this road I circle,
a *cingle*, for it meanders and climbs
the tall cliffs of caves cryptic with reindeer
in flight, herds of bison and horses, all etched
with prehistoric palette. Long ago, tracing
by firelight, some Neanderthal shaped a red
ochre belly to the stone.

What did he know?

That everything lost is simply lost
unless recalled in rock that rarely crumbles.
Last month, my friend put his head back
and died, holding cucumbers in his hand.
The ease of this leaving, a bird lifting
skyward, returns Montaigne's words:

be ready at any moment.

                                Perhaps the past,
like your name, can't be changed or
claimed, but think how clarity of heart
created the dark forms the primitive carved
and knowledge your young parents craved.

Instead

(for Pinkney)

Let me help you pocket a star
some night near Atherton School
or unhook the sliver of moon from
the tangle of leaves as we walk.

You don't have to run away.
We can step beyond school and rules
into solitude, the place of make-believe,
free from the calendar's wheels.

The world there is cosmic, edible,
fragrance of mint dances the paths,
its green scent astonishes the animals,
all who play in the circus of dreams.

It's the world of first times, spelled
out in the language of enchantment,
not the one lived day-to-day,
stuffed with disorder, family history.

I remember how wide the future was
when it was all imagination: a slate blue
lake that matched the climbing sky.
I know we can touch it with our hands.

Childhood

Maybe it hides
in the sprawl of abandoned toys
or the frayed pillow stored
in a closet corner, a place forgotten
by you, the twelve-year-old,
voicing your despair.

You can't be young again,
can't repair time's fabric
with a wish.
It was all so perfect
when you were three,
or even two.

Exiled now from Paradise,
the soothing sounds and touch,
you must wash your own hair,
scrub your teeth, even wear a bra.
No one carries you any longer
in the air.

Your desire's nourishment,
memory's cradle is balm
in the ache of growing up.
Maybe you guess that life
may bare us leaf by leaf,
branches exposed to sun's heat.

That I May Understand

> *If we had keen vision and feeling*
> *of all ordinary life, it would be like*
> *hearing the grass grow . . . and we*
> *should die of that roar which lies*
> *on the other side of silence.*
> —George Eliot

Lead me to the land you enter,
every time I question you:
the place planted with purple-leaf
plum trees, Japanese maples, and
rose bushes impossible to pass.
Take me through the pale wheat
filling your vision on the left and
right of me, just as it did when you
hid at two among white sheaves,
your fair-hair in perfect mimicry.

Like the wild child of Aveyron,
you never trusted your keepers,
following instead your passion
for freedom of the fields, always
crossing and re-crossing streams
to throw people off. In silence
you tended each earth pocket,
watched the chameleon change,
the bright world nested in

the savage blue of your eyes.
A man shaped of summer and grass,
you see past me to the wind's turn
in the trees. Someday I may find you
drinking out of rain pools, your nails
grown long, the network of veins in
your hands changed to the underside
of a leaf. Before you go from me,
tell me while I may still understand,
let me hear about the sylvan sounds
found on the other side of silence.

Remembering a Husband After His Death

I scratch out words on leaf, stone,
any sheaf of paper will do.
Grief scrawls across
the heart's cellar the call
to bring you back, say the unspeakable,
kneel at the crossroads
to the Beverly house
where you worked your crafts,
hammering wood, throwing pots
for others, or for me, oblivious
and eager to be free of sadness
that baked in the all-night kiln.

How can this pen spill out signs
of tenderness endangered as ours was then,
to salvage what became shipwreck,
breaking from stern to bow
the love we began when children ourselves.
It's impossible now
to empty cold lunchboxes, take back words
that wounded in that small kitchen
before history marched us here.
The sorrow I feared has come home,
refuses to let go,
its sound echoes this lament, love.

Sense

The body seeks touch,
silky rub of sheet,
like water slips along
the shoreline or the moon
caresses the windowpane.
Its light dissolves space
between, brings everything closer,
urges us to begin again
to lift the palm over the hushed
skin, a motion of cells
and self, finding the way
across the bridge
of this closed castle.

Layers of earlier rhythms
rest in the flesh of an arm's
turn, tilt of spine,
infused with song sparrows
and how sunlight once felt.
Like a cat licking its young,
each gesture carries succor,
a taste of the carnal.
It shakes you awake, this
staggering language of flesh,
opens the gate beyond
blemish and wound, weds
us to the fleeting world.

Grandmothers

Dead before we were born, grandmothers
are an October distraction of mind, like
tree leaves changing from soft green to
vermillion, then slowly withering as they
fall, tumble under the feet of those who
don't know the wisdom of grandmothers,
their forgiveness of blasphemies, the
God Damns, the *Hell* we fear we will go to
if we utter one word more; their readiness
to believe all, each story of acclaim we
make up as we aim for the heart which
we have won long before we were born.

IV

Art

Everything
here depends on relationships:
details touched by intimate light
so like the poet finding her song,
I know rapture is the true terrain.
— "Still Life with Music"

Tableau

What if ashes rained down on us,
a gray avalanche trapping our bodies
in their twenty-first-century chairs,
your spine sidling back in the seat,
an old book cracked open
against the edge of the night.
And me, curled next to my poetry,
blue sweatshirt for warmth, almost
asleep and beginning to dream.

Preserved for time without end,
this end-of-the-day scene, on view
in a glass room of a future museum:
two creatures encased in white calcimine,
ruined statues, arms or legs
broken off, anthropology
and physics now reconstructing
from stumps of stone, our inner lives,
the marriage of our bodies.

Only moments before, the ash
rushed in like the sea, drenching
each small thing in cinders; now
what we gave each other flourishes
in the glance of others, or it remains
the pale powder of dust and time;
your eyes seared blind for eternity,
my hair cast across the poems
like a frozen handful of straw.

At the Museum of Natural History: Reading Leonardo da Vinci's Codex

In this masterpiece of science,
the primary subject is water.
The brook taught da Vinci
to speak, repeating its sounds
in his reveries, rolling thoughts
in quick succession over slick rocks.

Da Vinci drew from these dreams
the map of the Codex, which opens
to the visible, each image lifted in
his mind's glass, written backward
with a mirror, its truths encoded.
Like water or the window case

we stand before, the manuscript
reflects, a lens lifting back another
world and our lives now: son grown
beyond mother, maple tree in
full flame punctuating the air with
rust, yellow. In this November

room we read the real to find
what is hidden, wondering
just how the lucent curve cradled
in the moon's crescent mimes
the light from earth's oceans;
or how da Vinci knew in 1510

that water flows through rivered
landscapes, like your blood
and mine singing an echo
of the pulse of things, often
flooding the heart before
finding its way to the sea.

Still Life with Music

(after Vermeer)

Nothing interrupts life so composed.
There's all the time in the world
to see this freshly made bread
wrapped in soft folds of cloth,

to feel earth's calls through
its baked grain and flowing spring
water, no longer remaining
in a burnished copper pail;

enough time to consider that
the silverware balanced at
the edge of a still life still
carries a taste of delicious loss.

Earth's gifts, human-made metals,
green tinted table and sky uncovered
in paint, disclose the real,
things in themselves. Everything

here depends on relationships:
details touched by intimate light
so like the poet finding her song,
I know rapture is the true terrain.

The Dance Of Darkness

All day it comes back to me, the grief
on each of their faces, two Japanese dancers
who carry their bodies as if they might spill.

The feeling is closest to a wave as it peaks
but never collapses, how each curves the body
toward the other without destroying shape.

They dance a language, this man and woman,
utterly spare, the Hiroshima dance of darkness,
where each step slides from the mold,

the hold that imprisons body. So the sorrow
lifts back to me in shades of dark and white,
in slow unconscious moves we make,

like this primordial pair, where despair
discovers itself in another body and beats so
near the surface, others see it as desire.

Schumann's Opus 21: Three Voices

I

London, May, 1856

Robert,

My hands sink into chords you taught me
to revere. I am delivered now
from the cradle, endless pregnancies,
the years of one piano, ever yours, within a house
future ages will name: Schumann's.

The sea grows dark; it strikes against the coast,
cleanses the chalky stone. It surged once
through the house, enveloped what
I'd make of motherhood, urged me to play
in spite of children, to take this music out.

Our lives are built on separation.
You are two years at the asylum, your fingers
to your lips, measuring breath and words.
Sixteen years and eight children,
our many works, now this pain.

Let this music mark how I do love you.
I play this as you would wish, boldly
with a strong mind. *How beautiful.*
I have prepared myself to be the woman I am.
The man I love dies mad at Endenich.
And I remain.

                                     Clara

II

Endenich, June, 1856

Clara,

Are you here?
You have come to play.
Play what London loved,
Strauss, a bit of Schumann.
I have made a keyboard
carved into my desk.
No key is missing, none out of tune.
I practice daily, oh, but play.

We have no need for sound, we two,
and do not weep, I beg you, no.
How beautiful, the sleight weight
of that small hand, the pliant wrist.

What I fear is mind that feeds itself
itself, which breeds without relation
to the past. I labor to be sound,
to force my mind to grasp what genius
you devote to me. Rivers run rich
between our souls, clear and brilliant,
like our years, our music.
They can't be lost, nor banished.

                            Robert

III
Bonn, April, 1897

Clara,

Can you see me
lingering behind this arc of cedars we set
to shield your grave from too much light.
Even your name carried its own brightness.
How could I outlive you?

Strange now to remember Robert's pose
as if a photograph after forty years.
We sat outdoors, smoked, talked,
his head inclining toward the sky. At dusk,
two cranes flew through low sun,
their wings moving slowly in flight.
At first he waived his scarf, summoning,
then he said: "*How beautiful.*
They pair, but once,
how beautiful," and he went in.

But you, Clara, in public, beguiling.
"If only," you told me,
"I could find longing as sweet as you do."
How seduction flattered me.
So I wrote such melancholy,
E major to be sure.

That bright and fragrant key,
a melody that moved toward
human sadness not quite entered,
seen only in fingers rising from the keys,
or felt in your best hours of love
barely shifted from him to me,
both of us desperate for his shattered mind.
"How beautiful," I remember,
"How beautiful, the throb along your temple."

                                        Brahms

Shape Dissolves into Color
(1840-1926)

Le Havre
waves sweep the tethered ships, luring him
out-of-doors to paint the consuming light,
each shift in sunrise a restless reflection,
luminous, as the fleeting moment
he captures in the harbor's hazy landscape
with strokes others later give a name.

Paris
students call him 'dandy', the penniless
painter with ruffled cuffs who studies smoke,
its swelling clouds stoked for him at Gare
Saint-Lazare, an unlikely spot for beauty
or fugitive whitecaps; his color floods nearby
houses with hues that do not fail to fascinate.

Rouen
Cathedral towers over the store window
where he sketches the facade, impermanent
it seems, colors converted by weather, sun,
each variation a shimmering veil, only a slim
reminder of structure, not substance or weight
of things; yet he will dream it falls on him.

London
fog surrounds the Houses of Parliament
in purple, dissolves the sun's gold,
all shapes smudge at century's birth,
even the building's a ghost any slight
breath could shake, and the horizon's edge,
filtered through space, bewitchingly blurs.

Giverny
water-lilies, wisteria, and jonquils blossom
into tangles of color in his backyard and link
like lyrics *en plein air* over thirty years.
At the end, almost blind, he still paints outside;
preserving his eyes with yellow glasses, he
brushes grass blue as the French cerulean sky.

Frida Kahlo Thinks of Death

Two serious accidents I suffered in life:
a streetcar that knocked me down
and the love of Diego.
There were others.
A withered leg, amputation, miscarriage,
and the old genius
of the Bolshevik Revolution,
his hand on my knee under the table,
scholar's glasses pleading for a sign.

But Diego festers in my breast
sharp as yucca, cactus milk leaks
from the nipple. He shows me what
it's like to be a woman, awakening
to longing that spreads like a stain
across the canvas, Oxacan blood
red rich as hibiscus, dragging
the body down, a single hand
closing above waves.

When I die, smoke from the kilns
on the easel by my bed will shadow
Diego's face, his lips only a smear
of ash. *Oh my Diego, don't grieve.*
I will pass through the oven door,
my hair flashing in rays, like a mantle
of light, a giant sunflower
framing my face. *A joyful exit.*
I hope never to come back.

Millais' Painting: Ophelia

for Elizabeth Siddal, 1829-1862,
wife of Dante Gabriel Rosetti

I

Her face too common, the woman with unlucky
red hair lies in the blue bath water numb,
her pale hooded eyes and ginger lashes
dismissed by the peaches-and-cream look
of Victorian time. In lucent nightgown
scattered with rosemary and rue,

Ophelia surrenders reason, or appears to,
floating, forsaken by her lover. Even the artist,
absorbed in her loosening hair, garments,
forgets the lamps warming the model
who lingers with little cover. Later Rossetti
will discover her as his Beatrice and wed.

II

Banned for her beauty and posing, the woman,
pupil to her husband, tried to paint. Her figures
stiff, sketchy, without limbs under their drapery,
lay bare an earnest brushstroke. Was the painting
mimicry of her lover's images or simply
rare and untrained? In art, perspective tells all

but what we know of her is a man's view:
a fragile face enshrined on canvas, slim body

reclining in postures difficult, spiritual,
and in Rosetti's poems buried in her hair,
growing, as if reaching for air after
seven years, when he dug up her grave.

Chest Pains: Weymouth Center for the Arts

Sometimes aches travel down the chest
after driving miles, and you ask: what
if I die here away from love, suppose
I lower the pen and my heart snaps shut.
Nothing's meant to last.

Think of the woman after
an evening bath settling herself
in a chair, saying softly
to her husband, I'm a little tired.
She never stands up again.

Maybe you've wondered what
would be left behind: torn scraps
of paper to cancel future dark,
drawers stuffed with letters, dirty
underwear, and soap—all perishable.

Perhaps you've given more thought
to this and said proper farewell,
a kiss on your daughter's forehead
or that lingering look across breakfast—
something you're not likely to do.

Most of us fear death will take us.
As I did, smashed to the ground
with a broken collarbone after running

a country road. Far from home, I lay
staring up at clouds, ominous, fleeting.
But this morning the world's given back
through the glass: pale sunbursts dotting the lawn,
last night's road white with open sky.
Unfamiliar and clean, like sudden rain,
everything leaps out, rinses my eyes.

Sexton

I met her once, just months before
she found forgetfulness, a Lethe-like
figure touching elixir to mouth,
fumbling the glass, the poem she read:

Live or die, but don't poison everything,

she said. Depend on no one, not
the wide empty sky, nor the distant moon.
No one will rescue you. We are our mother.
That's the only thing.

Reading Outer Dark

> *He wondered why a road*
> *should come to such a place.*
> *—Cormac McCarthy*

Here humankind appears half-literate, mostly animal.
A baby abandoned on a tree stump in night's cold
howls, his hands beating back the dark. Bare trees
stand, postures of agony in this garden of violence,
doomed like the human from the start.

This is what lays claim to our attention, sickness
at the core of things. 'Sick unto death,' Kirkegaard
might have said of this record of what life has done.
A landscape after epidemic plague, uncovering
a new geography. Or perhaps it is an old one.

The story unfolds a terrible homeland, not the fiery
traditional hell, but a haunting process of erosion.
Reading this is seeing something I've never seen
but always known, like a mark I find on my body,
not remembering just when and how it got there.

Uncertain

Certainties don't interest me much:
Ghana's road map shifting east,
then north, or signs that name each

arboretum tree, Baobab, Oak.
What really matters is something
other than direction or kind: a place

that pulls me from the creased route
where Africans boil strychnine bark in
a brew to test for truth: Here drink this,

they say. I can't help questioning what
I don't know. Didn't Heisenberg disturb
the universe with principled uncertainty?

So when I heard about a father leaving
the tropics, building a shipping crate
from wood to be used again, perhaps for

a bench or desk in America, I imagine
he built it for his two-year-old son who
wouldn't go without taking sea-battered shells

or stones found in sun-red sand, scarred
as if marks mattered. I think of the
son grown, leaning on a desk, memories

of an old existence engraved in its grain
and how I still, always, want the story
of what I can't keep or be certain of.

For in this story everything's uncertain,
facts unknown, questions still unanswered,
even in a world as composed as this.

After Paula's Death
Clara Westhoff Speaks

> *Clara Westhoff, sculptress, and*
> *Paula Modersohn-Becker, painter*
> *(Worpswede 1899 - 1907)*

Words never said,
perhaps not known,
or formed into thought,
linger on our eyelids
in that famous photograph
from which our husbands
are missing.

The gaze holds us
in time at Worpswede,
working in the same studio
your paint, my clay.
Never would we be faint-
hearted again.

Passion for art
offered freedom
for you to paint yourself
nude, full breasted,
each hand holding
a tiny, pink rosebud.

Yet critics said,
"it wasn't done.
Not by women
painters."

I like to think
whatever went unsaid
between us,
yielded to creamy skin
asking to be stroked,
touched it with a brush
of rose paint centered
in the flesh of nipples.

Kathe Kollwitz Sketches Her Son

Through the window Kathe Kollwitz
sees gray huddled shapes lined up,
a hand reaches for the doctor,
her tired husband, who beckons
in the white-lipped, trembling
woman and her child.

Whatever it takes. Hours without pay,
My husband will see them. His patients
teach me about lines, printmaking,
the world's distortions: poverty, hunger.
Just other names for injustice.

Kollwitz sketches women suckling
frail babies, the cold rooms
crowded, then she gazes into
the mirror, at her seven-year old
son enveloped by her body, her
thick hand drawing the circle tight.

No color. I will make powerful
lines on soft ground, distortion
must merge mother and son
into one.

In the glass: her own features, mostly
hidden, nose nestled in the child's skin,
taut lines of grief begin. Her breath
explodes, seems to swallow
his life back into the womb, birthplace
of sorrow, his, hers to come.

Intimations

(after a painting by Laurie Doctor, poet and painter)

Maybe it's the painting's timelessness
that provokes the painter who strokes
the wave of blue wash across a domed canvas.
For then she layers a curve of sunlight
between deeper blue sky and the sublunar
shelter, our human world, its body, arching
to receive the silent, cosmic downpour.

In this hemisphere of tiered light and air,
the earth, chrysalis of repose and flight,
becomes the ark, hospitable space,
for the one who sings of time's ocean,
the flavor of childhood. The poet opens
the window to the universe but knows
she scribbles on the back of time.

And what of these words in paint. Are they
ciphers of an unknowable ancient scroll?
The painter colors immutable rhythms of stars,
the poet hovers in the hollow of the flower, both
urgent to engrave in paint or to limn in pure vowels,
a new language. To speak at last from silence
folded in leagues of blue, the mother tongue.

We Stand Before Van Gogh's Last Painting

It's December in this city of waterways
where boats lift small sails in handkerchiefs
of bon voyage. Here in the Reiksmuseum,
Van Gogh's blue vibrating skies challenge
the overcast drab outside, the gray light
we abandoned, eager to recapture last
summer, the Arles green of cypress and olive.

For us, it's a return to light; for Vincent
it was a first finding. After the dark Dutch
peasant paintings, their smells of bacon,
potato steam, his pallet flamed with color:
wood, the yellow of butter; grass tinged
in bronze, and red oleanders, raving mad,
as others said he was then. Was that madness?

Or was it, as history suggests, nobility of soul
at odds with circumstance, or with
Van Gogh's own violent need for paint,
for choosing the wrong life each time.
Other passions spill across this canvas,
his last, the one we stand before:
Fields of Wheat Under Troubled Skies.

It is your favorite painting, not mine.
Perhaps, the center path turning into
the field does not end abruptly for you,
nor the menacing sky with its fleeing birds
disturb your natural rhythm. But the wheat
is much too ripe; the brooding storm threatens
me, and even you, with its inner torment.

Exhibit of Van Gogh in Blues and Greens

An open book, *Van Gogh In Farben*, on my desk
and across my heart, a memory: A New York
afternoon when I wasn't sure if our love could come
again, I studied the dark blue of Van Gogh's Iris.

Piercing stalks of green jutted between; some
had fallen down. A bronzed table caught them,
holding the vase upright as I was held before the paint.

I would faint, I knew. Only these flowers,
the blues in skies, grass, kept me walking
through the exhibit, pain wadded in pockets,
circling my eyes like his stars and moons.

But this morning I see color blaze across this page
under a brilliant yellow haze where *The Sower*
spreads life-bursting seeds in whites, greens.

Ancestors

> *for Juliana Heyne, painter,*
> *"Les Baux de Provence"*

It's a landscape Dante knew in another world.
A savage fist thrown high from earth, the ground
twisted into splintered stone, Les Baux sleeps
alone. An abandoned home of poets who sang
to any traveler or passing troupe, now a planet
whose spectral light hollows rock into palace
rooms where ancestral tapestries once hung.
Time and wind circle the crumbling stones
and the shadowed threshold you paint smoke-blue
squares into floor, like a shudder of memory.

Walls overflow the canvas with flesh-colored
amber before a brushstroke lifts them into ash,
a corner pooling as it does in the mind.
This painting illuminates the world, its lunar light
on falling stairs and broken boulders, the walls
 working loose of the ceiling of a dark past.
Everything here depends on connections,
this chance meeting of lineage with paint,
like a flute playing an ancient song,
with notes immutable yet lost.

Conversation at the Edge

> *On the verge of evening, nobody asks*
> *the dark where it came from, or who it is.*
> *—Jabes*

That night I learned about the body,
its unlocked window, how the ribs open
to the dark, hands ungrip, embrace
the quick taking as kindness, and how
you waited under unwaking sky,
still tending the body of what is left
in pictures and ink-scribbled papers.

Over the phone I heard your words,
lost tones familiar, sounds washed
with things unsaid, now recalled, even
called back, as I would wish to be
at the end, wanting possible passage
through this space swinging close
and dark as the air between us.

Outside, yellow leaves loving the earth
fell unseen, touched themselves to it,
soon to unite with rain in December shine.
Friend, I thought into the phone,
what enters the world as body is ripe;
what drops away is tendered by time.
Then as the black waves broke blue as
sky after rain, what I said was this:

Remember O'Keeffe's museum painting,
how she painted the clouds
white and flat as winding sheets
and how we lingered
before her jack-in-the-pulpit,
finding its pistil free from the cassock,
its glow like unstruck fire in a match head.

Meditation

If O'Keeffe's purple iris lifts its slim head
to the rim of awareness, beckoning
the spread of blue light on the horizon,
if the sunlight squared on the green rug
in Hopper's Brooklyn room creates compassion,
or the long note in a Bach fugue makes us think
about what was or might have been,
then we who search for resolution in the human
must paint evenings past and days that never were
with the brush of no regret and, in doing so,
sing of those we love, those who are present,
and those who remain pooled in memory,
each person a color burned into the canvas
of possibility, a lyric now heard.

V
Endings

Things vanish but I hold on.
Something within says, the moment
is worth keeping, protection
against the suck of infinity.
— "Survivor"

Survivor

Much of who we are is memory.
So I come here every day,
place of broken timbers,
torn plaster, rubble of the gone.
Yet here my mind is calm.
A crumbled photo buried in fine
gray sand the waves left behind,
a shattered glass, flattened toy.
Things vanish but I hold on.
Something within says, the moment
is worth keeping, protection
against the suck of infinity.

The past draws me back—
a shelled victim searching wreckage—
to know once again the sea's
scent from one lost summer
still radiant with touch,
the light of lived flesh.
This is the way of memory:
building up, then uprooting things,
trying to outrun ruin or
the panic inherent in being alive,
always caressing life's pictures,
record of its loss.

Finishing Touches

(for Karla)

Rehearsing for the day
you will drift from the room,
you are giving things away:
postcards become gifts
after years of familiar feel
and a thumbed book leaves
the past that held it.

Among life's notes
you remember your daughter
reading aloud from *Vogue*
to a dying grandmother she knows
—even unconscious—
will relish every color:
the fading light can't be blamed.

What fades falls:
the softening pear,
bruised apple,
and petals of autumn mum;
flavor of a sweet decay.

Even the body
who loves the world
that gave it fullness—
arms, breast, soft mouth—

will mellow someday.
So let tenderness raise
its clear sap
in tongues of song,
your mouth fill
with leafy richness,
scented with earth
you plant each spring.

Flowers will close
in a tightening whorl
and the long slanting days
pull you in. Cupped
in the warm lift of hills
only desire
will be left to tremble.

Confession

What I want to remember is how
it started late at night, words
breaking, like pearls chained
on a fragile thread strained
by the sudden gift of laughter;

three women spilling secrets,
confessing dependencies, flaws
they thought unnatural, unlike
the hole in the bird's nest,
the crack in the ice. These were

human imperfections, almost sin.
In one breath, they cast aside
instinct to hold the norm, those
formalities and blessings of day.
One told about gambling all night

in bright casinos; another smoked in
bolted bathrooms; and the third secretly
choked down candy. *Shared speech*,
my great-aunt might have said,
which meant the talk of people

reaching out and mingling,
each altering the other, as they
did, discovering falleness,
their friendship, and the possibility
that they might still be saved.

Arcadian

Each spring lilacs unbuttoned
their blue in the backyard
where the pine, once
an inside Christmas tree,
grew, hiding clouds
with shadow and scent.
Here you and I held solace in place
as the earth roots this tree,
with its swaying voice
and limbs lifting beyond
what can be seen.

Around the trees, bees hummed,
and breezes, almost breathless,
stirred the shaded air we shared,
tinged with eros and birdsong,
while the evergreen,
never a silent partner in our intimacy,
whispered: *There will be rain*
regular as a heartbeat;
loneliness, too.

I've come to understand why
Native Americans listen to talking trees
and Greeks told ancient stories
about a ship of special pine
whose crew had ears to hear its tongue.
I've learned how gardens fail us,
that the pine was never ours.
The scene echoed Eden: the tree,
all that enchantment, a fall.

The Past

What is there to say about this thick fog
slipping down, like a fisherman's net in
water, surrounding and pulling you along?

That it can fasten your heart to a sea
brimming with fear after the day's
heat or that a promised moment

tenses as the past comes flooding
home, little pieces of childhood in tow.
One second you are walking a dark lane;

the next one, you sink, your small body
turning in the blue-green water, gently
rocking, still descending, until your sister's

voice slams down on the surface, the panic
not reaching you yet, and she lifts you
by the head, the streaming hair into air.

Then you remember a day at Clear Lake:
lifeguards diving, searching the mud bottom
for a boy turned twelve, who has no sister;

he has not risen from play, and will not.
They kneel before him, almost pummeling
him to breathe, thinking don't die, don't.

But he has vanished from the flesh
they arrange with care, as if for long
voyage, or for a picture you still

carry in this fog, wishing you had a light,
like deep-sea fish have in their foreheads,
to negotiate the dark water of the past.

"So We Live Here, Forever Taking Leave"
after Rilke

Wherever I look these days
something is leaving.
The wispy ash grass, its green
lost to sun, sinks back to earth;
maples open handfuls of yellow and rust,
toss their farewell under the bushes,
across sidewalks still shiny
from dew withdrawing its shawl.
On a limb a nest breaks apart,
disappears at the touch time makes
on the way from one loss to another.

Now words are clusters of dry weeds
without nourishment or sense,
their sounds mimic melodies once
known, forgotten like a baby's babble,
pleasure's inflection outgrown,
worn by the world's seasons.
At night starlight leaves a little
of its dim past in a sky slowly
weathering black. Even in
my dreams since your illness,
I meet myself running away.

Holding

a mother speaks

When I rise from your bedside,
darkness I have held begins
to drift like night shadows

on snow, and frost spreads
a ghostly form across windows,
or when your young mouth winters

the test of speech, your legs twitch
with cold not felt, I try to remember
a world without leukemia and I can't.

When I hold your hand to my face,
I enter possibilities
destiny will not choose: the place

where a girl waits, looking
eighteen, hands grown slender,
opening to evening light,

as if to touch a world always
already there or to rescue
a little truth from our regret.

All the time we have left
holds this gesture,
and what you will never say.

Lives They Left Behind

> *In 1995, Willard Psychiatric Asylum closes*
> *after one hundred twenty-six years*

Four hundred twenty-seven suitcases numbered,
abandoned in orderly forms of decay
for decades. Their random sizes sit silently,
cradling contents. A hand-written marriage
proposal to Margaret Truman crumpled near

opened sheet music for *Moonlight Sonata*
and, thrown in a corner, silver-embroidered slippers,
never to dance again. One damaged bag contains
a scrapbook inscribed "My School Memories
in America," ends mid-sentence. Photographs

missing. The happiest hours of childhood doomed
to be forgotten, even a camera lens broken,
faded chauffeur's license, never renewed,
and folded notes, small tokens describing hope
confined to trunks and waiting half a century,

all life left behind, spent in custody.

Memory of a Student's Untimely Death

(for Jim Grote)

At times it seems strange, unexpected, the past
and who we were then, and what the mind lifts
back on an overcast sky in early May, when

bereft, we come to pledge faithfulness to you,
thick, grey clouds shifting overhead, wind
slipping through wet leaves as we rush into church

and come to a stabbing stop before a larger-than-life
photograph of you taken years ago, long hair
shaping your always curious face, that direct look

that met us in the classroom, only this time younger,
yearning toward a future no longer there, years
before you would become a scholar, spinner of stories.

Sometimes we need to be given back to ourselves,
like this photograph, an unexpected gift, to be
remembered, not as we are now but as we were

before the transfiguring wheel took its turn
with us and lines appeared like clockwork across
our hearts, before we knew the past was always

under revision, changing as we change, the way
our sadness and incomprehension can be converted
into reasons we can barely understand.

Pavane

Alive now for almost two centuries,
the giant, copper beech wears
a crown of ocher-red leaves
as a dead tree surrenders nearby
and falls into its outspread arms.
Embraced at last, rasping in wind,
the dead one will slowly carve a niche
in the living branch, shearing away
the rough outer flesh, revealing
the pale, inner bark. Year upon year
the dead tree will rub its broken body
against the living, building a mournful music,
making its raw mark, wearing the tough
bough down. Even as it flourishes its crown,
it will moan and bend, the deep bow sound
of the living shouldering the dead.

Promise

In today's news I read that
late in life--his eightieth year--
a dying man purchased a thick strip
of woods. Later the man cut
a trail with hedge shears,
built two bridges over rivulets,
and skirted the wild myrtle
in his journey down to a creek.

Perhaps the green of trees
beckoned him to slip
the confines of mind or he
wished to conquer flesh's fate
by living on, cutting through
the elusive promise of woods,
raspberry and rose brambles
stabbing the face and hands.

I imagine you this man,
—if you had lived.
Once in Africa you whacked your steps
through rain forest, cut bamboo stalks,
slim dark trunks, tied them at angles
with tangled vine,
creating a monument to impulse:

a jungle gym for a son to climb on.
Or the time you walked that son
miles to a forest maze of mounds,
earthworks made by humans long ago,
for reasons known only to them
and found the crushed fragments of a bowl,
leavings, fragile as old paper.

The same dream? An eighty year-old
man stumbling through the underbrush
and a younger you searching forest ruins
with a boy. Both of you hungry
for the singing light in trees
and thirsty for the ever flowing sap.

That Kingdom

> *Childhood is the kingdom*
> *where nobody dies.*
> —Edna St. Vincent Millay

Something not meant
to happen, happens.

From the top
of a sycamore,
a tiny starling falls;
the sun slants down,
honoring it.

In Japan an earthquake
shakes
generations to an early grave;
those left say *Syoganai*
as they bow
their heads:

There is nothing you can do.

That night you knew
the light we call stars
had traveled aeons until
now to falter on the field
where you left
childhood.

In silk of sorrow,
you buried a sister,
still longing
to live,
in stillness,
darkness.

Over wintering land,
in ways deep and sharp,
stars
you had watched
together
went out.

After the Death Camps

I

It goes on burning in your bones,
in your brain; years after, the smoke
still rises behind the walls, even on
May second, a birthday to liberate
all others. In Poland, though the water
from the stone well at Tylicz never ceases,
it never soothes the smoldering,
nor the fearful dreams fueling sleep.

II

For months a redwood tree may flame
the fire that consumes it, burning
a black scar to its core. Within the
burnt sepulcher, as if a miracle, seeds
bearing a young tree begin to green. Let
us sift the ashes for new life, for the story
forged in suffering, where the birth into
words is as terrifying as fire or love.

Earth Borne

Brick by brick, buildings flake
into ruin, a crude pot crushed,
scatters on the forest floor, but

along the Mississippi River where
we traveled, mounds shaped by ancients
into familiar forms, a bird or bear,

rise out of the ground toward sun,
outlasting everything. These burial sites
remain unchanged, unlike most things

of human making. For centuries Colombine
covers the woodland people
in common graves, not in lonely plots.

You and I are bird shadows, dry leaves
at dusk, who have seen these effigies,
as they were meant to be, from the sky.

Loneliness, we know, is flying
or dying alone, or it's one stone
shaking in night's hollow gourd.

So let us make a sacred bird
of dark soil and yellow clay from
the river bed, set out offerings of sage

and books for our heads, join hands
with rain and the coming moon; let us
lie down forever in all that flowering.

A Runner's Quarrel

Say I consider the mind/body problem
as Descartes did. I could dispute that fall,
my cut head, and what would undoubtedly
become a deeper pain in the arm. I might
doubt my own experience, those senses
that sometimes mislead, even deceive.

How well Descartes pruned the tree
of knowledge, each gnarled branch
pared, then smoothed by the press
of his thought, even a grown limb
splintered in one distinct moment,
I think, like that one.

Though it wasn't so clear lying
on the ground, my collar bone severed,
that the mind is more easily known than
the body. It's hard to believe that things
might not exist. The reality of a rock-
strewn road fractured senses

Descartes can't know as I do.
So I'll not argue with a day of rain
humid with pain and reason. I see
with clarity my body before falling and feel
how life ends. This bruise will blossom,
disappear like any withering tree, but once

death leaves its mark on the shoulder,
a stillness comes, the rain stops
and the sky takes its breath,
where for one moment, the world
refuses to be a dream and hangs
like a clump of red berries.

Timanfaya Lava Fields: Canary Islands

The faithful wind sounds like running water
where there is none, spills endless lament
across lava fields whose folded black quilts
bed down eleven villages. Centuries ago.

Perhaps a young boy, throwing off a blanket,
saw the earth open suddenly near Timanfaya;
mountains rose, spitting blood from wounds,
fouling the soil and air for days.

An island without storms; smoke clouds
and wrathful claps of thunder must have
urged him indoors, where the bright lapping,
like the sea he loved, might not reach.

This lunar landscape, Montanas del Fuego,
remains: a public park forbidding us to touch
or walk, we drive the one road allowed. Day
throws disbelief across the glass, filthy with ash,

and nameless presences press against the doors.
A boy can be extinguished like these cold stones,
but this wasteland's preserved, saved for viewing,
like a national treasure or the dead.

I shift the gray quiet in my clothes, think
about that boy, the sign that reads: *Don't Touch.
Subject to Human Erosion.* Past fury settles
on the skin, erupts each time the wind cries.

The Apple

> *Travel Back in Time Not So Far Out*
> *—New York Times*

I have Einstein to thank for this possibility
when he said gravity bends time and space.
Now offering complex mathematical probability

three scientists ignore the philosophical case
that travel backward in time will rupture
causality. They posit a worm hole as the place

of journey to past time. An ordinary traveler
proceeds like a worm crawling over an apple,
they tell me. But should space warp to the inner

core, a tunnel opens, childhood tumbles
into the air. There: the torn screen door and Mother,
I have come back to touch your eyelids, to stumble

through my life again. Yet I can't be the character
in a tragic play, the one who repeats it all,
for I know what lies in this return: the specter

of longing. Father, lover, each turned back, call
from the throat of time: let us restore
what's gone. Say I forget that sorrow is original,

loss at the bone. Forget direction even more
as theorists urge. But if true paradise is always one
that is lost, do I want to reach the apple's core?

What Is Found

> *"We have fallen into the mistake*
> *of living from our little needs till*
> *we have lost our deeper needs..."*
> —D. H. Lawrence

Speaking about mutual fears
all afternoon we worried
that deeper needs are being lost
to lists for bread and wine,
that world-weariness
smothers the bright flame
writers reach for in existence.

But few can live in such heat,
though some do and we try,
bringing the body's breath
to speech under these trees
shouldered together
in indescribable grace,
as if to comfort us.

Rather than search for words,
perhaps we can count on what
is here in this glen, wood fern,
and the land's green swells.
We might awaken to starlight
as it falls faintly over us
and what lies within our reach.

Afterword

My poetry embodies a central notion that I derived from reading Henri Bergson and Marcel Proust; namely, that imagination and memory counter external objects in the world with images of their own making. Moreover, both Bergson and Proust taught me that memory is changed by the imaginative spirit, even if the past is disappointing or tragic, that deep remembrance returns us to original feeling where we constituted ourselves and our world. At the same time, having lost all four members of my family by the time I was twenty, I was convinced I would die before I turned thirty. Deep remembrance offered me loss and death.

    The theories, however, attracted me, provided me with ideas and words to corner the emotions always lying in wait. A friend once told me I lassoed my emotions with words and transformed my feelings into poetry. In my writing on Virginia Woolf, I learned from her memoir that when she had a blow from behind the cotton wool of daily life, she would take it and turn it into words and it would lose its power to hurt her. Woolf also revealed that memory was the means by which an individual builds up patterns of personal significance within which she anchors her life and secures it against pain. All of these insights have an uncanny resonance with my life and in my craft. Death has laid a foundation in my life and become an insistent companion in my poetry.

    My past writing has been a repository of grief and a necessary step in the growth of my aesthetic, but central to my work now is present perception, living deeply in the present, disclosing being, and as Nabokov advised, "in caressing the details, the world comes streaming back, alive and real." In *Speak, Memory* he tells us : "This is ecstasy, and behind the ecstasy is something else, which is hard to explain. It is like a momentary vacuum into which rushes all that I love. A sense of oneness with sun and stone." In writing my poetry, I hope to find that oneness with sun and stone and offer it to others.

    This collection of poems, entitled THE CRUEL RADIANCE OF WHAT IS, takes its title from a line of James Agee's *Let Us Now Praise Famous Men* and a quote from Virginia Woolf prefaces the poems:

> To look life in the face, always to look life in the face, and to know it for what it is, at last... to love it for what it is, and then to put it away.
> *To the Lighthouse*

Acknowledgments

Many poems in this volume have appeared in the following books:
- *Country of Light*, Mount Olive College Press, Mount Olive, North Carolina, 1998
- *What Vanishes*, Arable Press, Louisville, Kentucky, 2006

New poems have appeared in the following anthologies and journals:

Virginia Center for the Creative Arts Anthology: Celebrating Forty Years of Poetry, October 2012
- "After the Ice Storm"

Imagine This! An Artprize Anthology, Greater Lakes Commonwealth of Letters Chapbook Press, Vol. II, July 2014
- "Tableau"

The Louisville Review
- "Conversation at the Edge" (v. 80, Fall 2016)
- "Shape Dissolves Into Color" (v. 80, Fall 2016)
- "Spawning the Space" (v. 80, Fall 2016)
- "Paris Light" (v. 79, Spring 2016)
- "That Kingdom" (v. 79, Spring 2016)
- "Evolutionary" (v. 79, Spring 2016)
- "Ache" (v. 79, Spring 2016)
- "If/Then Meditation" (v. 78, Fall 2015)

Open Twenty-Four Hours
- "After the Death Camps" (2016)
- "Pavane" (2016)
- "In 1995 Willard Psychiatric Asylum Closes" (2016)
- "Memory" (*2015*)
- "After Clara's Death Paula Westhoff Speaks" (2015)
- "Intimations" (2015)

Asheville Poetry Review
- "Sense" (2004)

My deepest thanks to Sena Jeter Naslund, mentor and friend; Molly Peacock, Rachel Hadas, Betty Adcock, Stephen Dunn, C. K. Williams, Karla Shanahan, Susan Bentley, the Six Voices poetry group: Quinn Chipley, Laurie Doctor, Misha Feigin, Ky Li, Steven Skaggs, and Pat Owen for insight in the writing of these poems.

Without the friendship of many others, the poems would not exist; in particular, let me thank Melissa Day, Elaine Wise, Dale Stover, Marcia Gealy, Suzette Henke, Kim Jonason, Judy and Steven Lippmann, Mary Ann and Robert Stenger, and my Chinese and American graduate students who inspire me on this journey. My gratitude to you all.

Residencies at the MacDowell Colony, the Weymouth Center for the Arts, the Virginia Center for the Arts, especially in Schwandorf, Germany, as well as support from the New Jersey State Art Council, the North Carolina State Art Council, and the Kentucky State Arts Council have contributed to the book's creation as well. For help with the manuscript I am indebted to Ellyn Lichvar, managing editor at *The Louisville Review*, and Quinn Chipley, meticulous reader and friend with sage advice.

Finally, I thank my philosopher husband, Osborne Wiggins, for his gift of words, and our children, who are irreplaceable in our hearts for everything that matters.

You all have made these poems possible.

Author Note

Annette Allen is the author of two books of poetry (*Country of Light*, which received the Lee Witte Award, and *What Vanishes*, which was awarded the Dr. Guy Award by the Winston-Salem Arts Council). A MacDowell Colony Fellow, she is the recipient of three statewide arts council poetry awards, and recently, a Poetry Fellowship from the Kentucky Arts Council for 2018-19. Her poetry has been nominated for a Pushcart Prize and her work has been published widely in small presses, such as *Boulevard, The Louisville Review, Poet Lore* and in poetry anthologies. Other honors include an International Residency in Germany awarded by the Virginia Center for the Arts and two NEH summer fellowships. Former Director of the Doctorate in Comparative Humanities and Professor of Comparative Humanities at the University of Louisville, Allen also writes scholarly essays on women poets as well as medical humanities. She co-edited her latest book, *Clinical Ethics and the Necessity of Stories*.

More Praise for Annette Allen's
The Cruel Radiance of What Is: Selected and New Poems

Reading Annette Allen's newest collection *The Cruel Radiance of What Is* is like crossing a sharp mountain arête guided by a distant "flickering night light." On either side of the ridge are deep valleys, one shaped by darkness, the other saturated with light. The poems present vivid stories of the losses and longings attached to being mortal; and the deep desire to understand what might bring to light the darkest fears. Allen's technique is simultaneously reportorial and poetic. She brings to the poems clear thinking, a lifetime of deep learning, an exquisite use of language, and endless imagination to explore the uncertain and inexplicable, to answer the ultimate questions of existence. This collection is mature and important. I walk this arête with the poet, treading carefully, sharing her hope that the flickering light in the distance is attainable.

Maureen Morehead
Kentucky Poet Laureate 2011–2012
author of *Late August Blues: The Daylily Poems*
and *The Red Gate*

In *The Cruel Radiance of What Is*, Annette Allen returns to the past, its "distance," only to foreground it once again in the present, often through "touch," always through the sensual sound-work of her lines, their "rhythms of ache and refrain." In lovingly crafted poems that hope "to trap the unnameable," some of them homages to visual artists, composers, and writers, Allen leans toward "a larger lyric," personal and inclusive, memorable and moving, and full of feeling in its formal gestures. Allen knows that "rapture is the true terrain," and poem by poem her book creates a radiant landscape in which we can live, despite cruelty, in tenderness and affirmation.

Michael Waters
author of *The Dean of Discipline* and *Celestial Joyride*

Annette Allen's poems both discover and create imagery that lifts the quotidian and the sorrowful into a kind of radiance. If loss is the subject of much lyric poetry, as it is in these poems, the antidote is language that redeems: "Didn't the water seem to love/ the forest stretched across its body . . . " Allen's voice carries us through many kinds of loss and back into the light. She does it with striking images and earned wisdom.

Susan Ludvigson
author of *To Find the Gold*
and *Everything Winged Must Be Dreaming*

With depth, warmth, and a piquant play of detail, Annette Allen's splendid volume of new and selected poems, *The Cruel Radiance of What Is*, richly fulfills a life's work in poetry. All the contradictions and ambiguities of her title, both brilliance and the possibility of harm, vibrate with what it means to be alive in these readable—and re-readable—poems. "I met myself running away," Allen, a runner herself, admits, pulling us into her poems, her perceptions, even as they enlarge our own. Erudite but casual, moving and knowing, Allen spans lifetimes and places and eras from girlhood to womanhood, from Iowa to Paris, from a concert hall to a cave. What a treasure box of a book!

Molly Peacock
author of *The Analyst* and *Cornucopia*

In one of Rilke's letters he says that the true test of the value of a work of art is whether or not it arose from necessity. In Annette Allen's clearly voiced and beautifully crafted book, *The Cruel Radiance of What Is*, even the elegant five part structure (I. Place II. Light III. Family IV. Art V. Endings) suggests the essential themes and the clarity of vision she offers her readers. Weaving strands of daily experience, deep memory, rapture, and lament with a rich background of philosophy, music, and art, she has written a book of necessary poems

Greg Pape
Montana Poet Laureate 2007–2009
author of *American Flamingo* and *Four Swans*

www.ingramcontent.com/pod-product-compliance
Lightning Source LLC
Chambersburg PA
CBHW070428010526
44118CB00014B/1954